Title:	LOVE IS LIFE
ID:	4305224
ISBN:	978-0-615-26149-2
Category:	Poetry
Description:	"LOVE IS LIFE" a book written by Geoffrey Hyde, was influenced by an award winning poem "Love is Life". At an early age, Geoffrey has found the ability to share his feelings and thoughts with originality in written expression. This book is a full plate leaving you touched and moved in ways thriving to read it over and urging to pass it on.
Copyright Year:	© 2008 by Geoffrey Scott Hyde All rights reserved International Copyrights Conceived, written and illustrated by Geoffrey Scott Hyde
Language:	English
Country:	United States
Keywords:	Poetry Poems Poet

"LOVE IS LIFE"

love is life life is you
without my love life won't do
as sweet as honey my love is true
no one else only you
a blossom of rose or even two
its me its you
somethings gotta give but not without you
my feelings for you are way passed due
something not said or wrong words won't do
time and space only a waste
knowing my place is here with you
knowing what we have is already true
turning your back I wish you knew
sitting alone I'm now without you
love is our race set to our pace
only together we win this race
one glance is all it took
take a look life lessons writing a book
grab my hand lets dance
passing by each awkward stance
with only a glance
our love is life filled with romance
Life is love love is you
Always and forever my heart is for you

"REALISM IN A DREAM"

Life death beginning end
first last not pretend
walk run around the bend
turn the corner see the end
fast slow think go
clocks tick legs kick
step after step memory quits
no sound just ground
flowing going running kicking
forward we go up up
breath after breath
the heart pumps
blood flowing eyes glowing
hair back road black
yellow stripes white lines
cars passing music blasting
leafs fall trees tall
air flow head low
breath blow wind slow
just go run breath sweat wipe
feel the sore the rain shall poor
win the fight keep it tight
don't slop don't drop
step after step stand up hands clinched
arms pumping mind on aint this something
a runners high passing by
some collapse some die
a race for life or a race to try
preparation now the test
some crawl some brawl
many around collapse and fall
tri athalon man stand tall
you beat em all
enjoy the moment and clap of each persons combining hand
enjoy it now this is your moment.

"LIFE IS WHAT HAPPENS WHEN WE'RE BLINKING OUR EYES"

The sun shinning weather warm
been here before this has never been worn
what a new day so begin to play
find myself seeking a new way
but in all reality its just a new day
I seek to go but decide to stay
run around this old town
young but shown an old frown
shown a smile lovely woman beautiful gown
making me ponder thinking looking around
always seeking but nothing found
on all fours I hit the ground
lay and sweat I roll around
grass blades sun and shades
upside down this is all a maze
going through this life one phase
or maybe its sweet like a pastry glaze
oh the good old days
maybe I'm dizzy and this is all a daze
the sun is out now settles and fades
taking off the sun shades
today was one of the most beautiful days
took a photo but nothing stays
now I stay or change my way
find a church and begin to pray
settling in the old fashion way
going to sleep drifting away
this is no ground hog day
life is short but not in this way
cherishing each dance each glance
each situation fast forward into a trance
standing tall in a stylish stance
holding hands wood lead paper and romance
writing thinking pondering staring out the window
seeing a boat I continue to write
smooth sailing water under now a float
passing by each country counting goat
leading this life feeling so remote
no one around no sound
nothing to seek nothing found
writing breathing thinking acting
somethings spilled wheres my napkin
no plans no faults just living with out defaults
expectations generations
families and memorizations

poetry poems sounds and oh mans
purpose intentions reasoning beyond our own damns
creation destruction justice and obstruction
meeting after meeting day after day
what to write what to say
shall continue to live this way
question after thought action now bought
put it on wear it and flaunt
feeling good and what not
smelling fresh looking best
now reached land
palm trees hot white sand
wind blowing and fanned
applaud me now I'm a new man
my trip is done it was so much fun
we can dream to live or live our dream
go up hill or float down stream
make it all easy or hard and mean
its up to us and our self esteem
uphold it now or change the theme
because in all reality dream a dream and live it well or fuck it all and go to hell.

"TODAY IN THE CITY"

Buildings high rises
full moons sunrises
men women hidden disguises
soccer games first place prizes
birthday wishes bring surprises
afternoon day arises
white lies and despises
telling truth seeing eyes
is turning around shooting dices
gambling style Miami vice
is eating pork with white rice
is dying in silence without advice
is turning our back on our own revises
scratching our heads finding lice
is burning away fire and ice
is melting away another day
is beginning a new another way
is fun when won than nothings done
is good when bad till one turns sad
happy and glad never mad
cant complain lets play this game
just curious will this lead to fame
maybe a title to ones own name

maybe own my own domain
burry the love feel no pain
washing away an old blood stain
the clouds above it begins to rain
just another day standing in between buildings and high rises
full moons and sunrises
looking around seeing men women hidden in disguises

"NINETY DEGREES"

I close my eyes I shut off sound
tilt my head back roll it around
onto my toes leaning off ground
forty five degrees no one around
man above seeing one below
burst of wind breathing it in
sun beams window seams
men and women live endless means
dare to live our dying dreams
fast but slow letting it go
arms spread lets go
clothes fill with air feeling naked and bare
blowing back my young hair
relaxed with out care
blessed with out fear
sun is out dry to a drought
see it feel it before times out
slow I know I'm letting everything go
one last breath deep but slow
that was then this is now
out I go head to toe
open eyes memorize
life highlights flashes of best days nights
loved ones eyes voices and pictures star in the skies
laughter and moments passing by
fast but slow I feel it all go
open my eyes who would know
tears come down wind shall blow
passing falling down I go
behind me now it begins to snow
midair turn to show
face to god he shall know
one last kiss to my lips
bliss a snow flake frozen to a lake
lips turn red now to blue
back hits first now I'm with you.

"FEVER"

One two three four five six seven eight nine
ten nine eight seven six five four three two one none
as I wake I'm missing all the fun
what was won now is none
early morning and late nights
counting sheep under the sheets
rolling around in bed
words thoughts million miles per hour running through my head
fan circles above eyes stare looking so dead
it's hot it's humid too weak to be fed
window open traffic and noise
memories of cars and little toys
girls and little boys
I sweat the clocks tick the fever kicks
the stomach twists everything spins
but only hot humid air winds
dreaming I'm growing fins
sinking beneath and swimming in water bins
buckets of shark soup made of fins
China Hong Kong pennies in copper tins
rain drops and strong winds
stylish kids fast cars always wins
bright lights neon and hyper whites
tricks and fire lights
into the nights
slow fast movement in motion
swaying flowing all on ocean
walking on water all these sounds of unknown laughter
floating above sky high
taking off feeling high
chills stomach light tickles in freight
fly with control low and high
seeing and knowing like a doctors eye
over the cemetery if I don't wake
I shall lye
falling now I hit the ground
open up my eyes beautiful sound
looking seeing lips so round
I was drifting all above falling now beneath the ground
feeling lost but awake now found
long lashes big eyes round
dark hair long thighs
rose scent glowing uplifting eyes
heavens near or already here
I awake to find this beautiful sunrise

seeing beyond starry skies
awake in a dream still dreaming what I thought was truth realize were all lies
living nightmares and dreams is no surprise
life is what happens when were blinking our eyes
live it now we don't get out with our lives
born to live end it when it dies
dreams truth and white lies
separate it all to realize what flys.

"DRIVE"

To live to die or die to live
sleep in or crawl out the crib
set it in sit it back
comfortable now lets begin our nap
short but sweet we awake on our feet
open the door do it once more
key ignites motor and lights
turning up the beautiful sound
wheels on ground
trance is dance
when driving is love and romance
fast but smooth under control
fast faster fastest
zoom zooming
moving cruising others on road look like there snoozing
this is living to die while they die to live
we rest our souls dreaming free and alive
destination no where just making it is somewhere
each day I drive is honey from a hive
to which you achieve to revive
dangerous but true its ones own life
live it to live feeling to die or die to live and always cry now fuck it and drive.

RAVE

Tall and skinny aint that pretty
looking laughing what a pitty
goose bumps punks and monks
sitting mixing orange and black
cut up pant with silk wrap
heavy metal while we nap
lost confused upside down
abused and used in between 2 worlds
one line one foot in one foot out
mouth open one eye wide I begin to scream and shout
half of me to sit and pout
one side rain the other a drought
turn it up or throw it out
read it write it burn it and put it out
thoughts in mind rehearsing all the time
heaven hell good and bad
outcast outlast
live now or already past
by your side or run and hide
put it all on stride with pride
all at once
what last is vast is fast is mass to adjust in a water glass
sun light all white into the night alright
live free but after one fight drop the glass shatters a splash
a tall drink of water or a broken glass
black night its bright
feeling new orange stains card board games
black and white funny faces and unknown names
music loud bumping into the crowd
turning spinning off the ground
jumping humping silent no sound
break dancing fans prancing
house hopping foots stomping
lights popping bulbs breaking
ears aching feelings faking
numb now it's a painting
in motion flowing like ocean
all mixing what a dangerous potion
a notion a feeling of life and devotion
on one day in a weird way but hush you don't have to say
you're brave so rave.

DANCE

Trying to remember what we chose to forget
you dance to remember while I dance to regret
something later to remember or something new to forget
what is life without lessons and regret
a journey of life tickling at each bet
laughing crying pants wet
moments and memories
asleep awake in and out
off and on
sad happy
dead or alive
we live today tomorrow revive
rebuild regroup
not in a circle or even a loop
off the track out of bounds
out of the box past the rocks
on the edge slipping falling
nails gripping hands slipping
life is chaos when perfect images distorted
perfection ending ripples and dimples
only to where it started
a lake below my hands let go
reflection of perfection who will know
deep I sink exhale and blink
questioning dreams pretty in pink
back to where I started afloat
above on back clothes spread
a flower on a wet lap
legs wide I glide
arms out sun shinning
blue skies cliff rise
others hop a rain drop
small to big they land a flop
right and left ripples and dimples
surrounded we splash and grasp
back to the wall we climb to top
lean now again we drop
all at once dancing are way down
deep beneath to touch ground
turning twisting upside down
hair wet clothes soaked

legs soar nails have broke
pinned to the wall I begin to choke
wrestling dancing under water romancing
I gasp I grasp I clasp and outlast
pretty in pink no more need to blink
eyes closed dark as night
picture the stars or pretend we jumped from mars
it's a rush a feeling of living
risk of love is to dance with out thought
to go with the flow and just let go
off a cliff or sink to the bottom now kiss and dance.

FIRST DAY

Chills bumps spider veins
red hands pale skin cold wind
metal polls unknown roles
first day what to say
standing still corner hidden back stiffened
where are the cubbies
freckles untied shoes
crooked pants stained shirt
hair combed flat still wet
skin dry face red need a nap
what is this place announcing my own name
this is so stupid lets just play a game
laughter in air kids stare
we hit the floor than jump off all four
feet running to the door
single file this took a while
out we go off we are
recess or lunch is all we hope for
reading writing coloring cleaning
early days early nights
growing and not sleeping barely even eating
no time no thought just in and out
off and on start and stop
now look back when did this all start
when did it end
memories pictures
 stories and videos of the first day that now is so far away with nothing left to say.

CHOICE

The more you push and chase the more they will rebel one must let go with love to which is an action expressing care a move that shows one shall always be there giving chance to let out what is within deep down to which is something wanted very badly hopefully to change for the better or possibly for the worse can only be felt this way and to trust is to give trust to believe in trust to give chance with out regret and if expectations are not met it is not a question that one shall forgive and forget but a question of understanding so to that one can accept what has happened to take a mistake or wrong doing a focal point to look with in see why what has just happened and to find way to compromise and understand is to learn and show intention to never make that single mistake ever again how ever life is a journey so unexpected filled with evil and good pushing and pulling temptations desires testing discipline as ones behavior only changes over time good advise and experience may make one wise but nothing can make one do something unless it is wanted deep down as we all live the life we chose we all have a choice to make situations will only better us if we put ourselves where we see ourselves as to say there is no other choice or option is to find excuse and reason is creating effortless and careless behavior because one can not face reality and accept things for what they are to which at any point is never to late to change but would rather escape reality until one day it will all become overwhelming most likely suppressed in unhealthy ways so one must realize the truth feel it recognize accept and speak it loudly to oneself or another in order to make a change in any direction this can be advised with assistance but only one wit in has control of there own life and the decisions they make to lead the life they live is only something done right with no regret few mistakes as the desire to do so is fully compromised understood and wanted wit in and let out as ones nature must be tested exposed in order to develop to be free and near perfected clearly understood to let out true nature and situations with in something wanted something thought of separating right from wrong and good from bad are choices we have but the path we chose is the life we live the journey we go on it is something that must be wanted understood having the ability to see and think clearly to make fair healthy decisions will determine ones happiness and choice to be true or suppress the truth hidden deep away from reality suppressed in unhappy fulfillment so be true be strong face reality and live now the choice is yours how you live is up to you stop and think it is never too late start now

IN THE KITCHEN

I love to come up behind you
With a kiss I shall surprise you
I love to hold your hips
As you pull my finger tips
Face to face your lips so red
The curves they do endow me
Chills upon your shoulder
As I caress and hold her
Hand in hand together we stand
Together growing older
Body to body oh so warm
I feel your tummy oh so round
I love and lift you off the ground
Into our room we shall lay
My head to your stomach I will pray
Our baby is on the way
I will never go
I will always stay
No words or actions ever
Please don't go away
I am your man forever
Another lady never
No excuses what so ever
Im really not that clever
You and I a family now
Lets focus on the matter
In the kitchen together
Gripping hands mixing batter
Our love and life shall never shatter

WINTER NIGHT

The sounds of metal blades skating on ice
A beautiful lake frozen by dawn
The sun rising ice cycles melting
A drop of water hitting the snow
The swans in white a beautiful sight
Bundled up kids wrestle and fight
Snow balls snow forts all through the night
Mugs of hot cider mugs of hot cocoa
Whip cream and warm apple pie
Pumpkin pie and sweets towering high
Adult's kids strangers shiver in laughter
Looking into a snow globe this would all look like a platter
Shake it up turn it around put it back down what do you see
A winter night and life so bright staying warm with laughter

TO JUDGE

Why must one be judged
Why must one be tested
Why must one be compared
Why must one be right or wrong
Why must one be stared upon
You live I live we live our own way
Each and everyone with something else to say
Me or you you or I looking with a different eye
A guy a gal a woman or man each with different lines on hand
The way you think the way you act is different what's wrong that
Originality compatibility versatility and mobility
Fitting in all alone outcast and unknown
What is normal if we are all sheep
What is right if one rebels
One wolf in the wrong herd
Some too cool to be with a nerd
Always be true being yourself
No matter what is judged let it all out
Do not be afraid try and continue
No matter what is said don't let it beat you
Judged by them or judged by you we are judged to better us

"A WAY TO LIVE"

FOCUS ON WHAT REALLY MATTERS
PURSUE YOUR DREAMS NEVER STOP
LIVE TO LEARN NO REGRETS
FIND YOURSELF
LIVE NOW WE DON'T GET OUT ALIVE
NEVER BE AFRAID TO TELL SOMEONE YOU LOVE THEM
CHERISH LOVED ONES
CARE FOR THOSE WHO CARE FORGET THE REST
BE TRUTHFUL AND TRUST WILL COME
BE GOOD AND GOOD WILL COME
TRUST YOUR FEELING DEEP DOWN
DON'T BE AFRAID
STAND UP TALL HEAD HIGH SPEAK LOUD
WHAT WOULD GOD DO NOW THINK WHAT YOU SHOULD DO
BE ABLE TO DO THIS IN FRONT OF FAMILY AND GOD OR DON'T DO IT AT ALL
FAIR GAME
BE CONFIDENT NO MATTER WHAT
LOVE UNCONDITIONALLY
MARRY FOR LOVE AND TRUST HAPPINESS WILL COME
DIE TO LIVE
NEVER HOLD BACK EXPRESSION IS HEALTHY
FORCE A SMLE AND A LAUGH
HUGS KISSES MAKING WISHES
DON'T BE AFRAID TO SAY I'M SORRY
DON'T BE AFRAID TO SAY I MADE A MISTAKE
LIVE LIFE WITH AN EXCLAMATION NOT AS AN EXPLANATION
SURROUND YOURSELF WITH GOOD PEOPLE
BE YOURSELF DO WHAT YOU DO LET THE NATURE WITH IN OUT
LET GO WITH LOVE
PATIENCE IS A VIRTUE
SEEK AND BE FOUND
DON'T WAIT TOO LONG
LOVE THE LIFE YOU LIVE
LIVE THE LIFE YOU LOVE
NEVER STOP BELIEVING
TRY AND YOU WILL SUCCEED
FORGIVE AND ACCEPT
POSITIVE CHANGES
GOOD INTENTION

SET THE BAR HIGH
GO FOR IT JUST DO IT
COMPLETE IT
COMPLIMENT IT
LIVE WITH MORALS AND VALUES
ALWAYS BE RESPECTFUL
EXCUSES PREVENT GROWING LEARNING AND THE TRUTH SO DON'T HIDE
CHERISH THE GOLD AND DIAMONDS IN YOUR LIFE HOW ABOUT FAMILY & A
HAND FULL OF FRIENDS
USE WHAT THE GOOD LORD GAVE YOU IN A HEALTHY POSITIVE TRUTHFUL
AND PRODUCTIVE WAY
NEVER BE AFRAID TO STOP WHAT IS WRONG TO DO WHAT IS RIGHT AT ANY
POINT AND TIME IN LIFE
GO TO CHURCH OR FIND TIME TO PRAY
INTAKE GOOD HEALTH IN EVERY POSSIBLE WAY
PRACTICE WHAT YOU PREACH
DO NOT CONTRADICT
GET IT ALL OUT
HOLD ONTO WHAT YOU GOT IF IT REALLY MATTERS FUCK THE REST
LIVE FOR TODAY TOMORROW AND THE FUTURE NOT FOR JUST ONE
IF NEEDED TAKE A STEP BACK
SLOW STEADY FOCUS
TAKE IT AT THE PACE THAT WORKS BEST
DON'T BE AFRAID TO START OVER
JUSTIFY
FREEDOM
BE SAFE AND TAKE GOOD CARE OF YOURSELF
RISK WHAT ITS WORTH
GIVE IT YOUR ALL AND BE HAPPY WITH WHAT YOU GOT OR DON'T COMPLAIN
NEVER BE AFRAID TO SAY I DON'T KNOW
ASK QUESTIONS
FIND ANSWERS
GET COMFORTABLE
WE ALL HAVE A CHOICE
CHOOSE THE LIFE YOU LIVE
 LIVE THE LIFE YOU CHOSE
LOVE THE SKIN YOURE IN
STOP AND THINK
PUT YOURSELF WHERE YOU SEE YOURSELF
START NOW ITS NEVER TOO LATE
VALUE YOURSELF BODY MIND AND SPIRIT
NEVER GIVE YOURSELF AWAY
SEX IS EXPRESSION OF LOVE TRUST ATTRACTION AND CARE CHERISH THIS
COMMITMENT IS NOT A JOKE
MARRIAGE IS SERIOUS NOT A GAME

*LEAVE BEHIND WHAT DOESN'T MATTER PICK UP AND START WITH WHAT
DOES
GET WHAT YOU NEED THAN WHAT YOU WANT
BALANCE COMPROMISE COMMUNICATION AND UNDERSTANDING IS KEY
ALWAYS BE RESPECTFUL*

"Ship Wreck"

*Talking dancing selfish romancing
standing sitting endless forbidden
hot air sweaty skin
open the window let in some wind
we sit we stare in an endless glare
each stance each glance is love and romance
each motion each notion is expressing emotion
love care a risk or dare truth beware
up down its all around hidden beneath or above the ground
something we seek when found slow fast like the speed of sound
the speed of light blowing by each day and night
some days we sit we talk we fight
some days we sit button after button remote into the night
the flash the sound of tv all around
escaping stretching opening our mind
to refine what was lost with loves divine
the balance of nature and mankind
creating the best and worst of ones own mind
sometimes making everything blind
we don't see we don't hear we don't fear
sitting at the tip of the ship with no one to steer
when speaking when sneaking in silent means of reaching
is not right for the fight or to make it right
its out of fear and fright to which despite is never right
so face the fear face the mirror
open up and let everyone hear
away from the tip and begin to steer
swaying and waving towards each persons rear
to open up the ear to let out what is far is now so near
keep going don't stop when you're there you'll feel every drop and every pop
as the ship sets on top of the beach end where it begins to drop
down the ropes off the plank out of the holes beyond the water bank
we sit here feeling where a ship once sank
the deep blue sea and mystery beneath
love is endless is wreck less*

like a large ship set to sea to fetch us
with no direction or prediction
storms above with lightning so frightening
thunder wind close your eyes
it all becomes dim a new day
a new way with only good things to say
on a sunny day where the ship has set
the beach is dry but the water wet
we open our door
talking dancing selfish romancing
standing sitting endless forbidden
hot air sweaty skin open the window let in some wind
is it real or all pretend.

"Perfect Song"

music in my ears eyes showing tears
no one around me not even my pears
the sound hides the little fears
but I wish we could cruise to this
I wish we could make dinner and just groove to this
I wish I could hold you close and just move to this
I wish you could lean in and we could kiss to this
hop in a boat and just float to bliss
but with out you here all the moments you miss
so I close my eyes and try to ditch the wish
but you and that feeling I hate to miss
so never give up and continue to wish
open my eyes damn you walked out to this
knowing this all you seemed to ditch all this
making you miss all this like a melted swiss Hershey kiss
but I wont stop just continue to wish
music in my ears eyes showing tears
no one around me not even my pears
it's the softest song saying nothings wrong
I wish it wasn't like this for too damn long
because with you it makes the perfect song
and you being here baby nothings wrong
but right now I hear the song
realize that youre gone
saying to myself I need to be strong
and live like nothings wrong
and hope it fades
but I wish we could hold on before its too late

not too fall end the wait
be who we are like on our first date
I wish you felt the love and believed in our fate
but right now its all open and out of the crate
so I sit and wait refuse to date
I don't want to ruin my love and your mate
because new moments with others we would only hate
no need for that so let me just continue to wait
I know that our love is no debate
so don't begin to question or test the fate
come back home I need to make love to you and hear you moan
I need you by my side not out to roam
music in my ears eyes showing tears
no one around me not even my pears
the sound hides the little fears
don't hide because with you by my side
we can live a life to a perfect song
so take that off and put something else on before our love is all gone

"Cinnamon"

tell me all your doubts let out all your poughts
ill comfort you till you cry to a drought
see the sun now experience fun
cuz thats all i really want for us hun
wake up in the morning to uh nice cinnabon
sugar coated till you feel bloated
a little cinnamon to relax a man
crawl under a warm blanket
imagine the warmth
the fireplace here
only a space to lay our face
side by side holding each other soft and close
and than pop up goes the toast
drop some honey spread some butter
sprinkle cinnamon because it all helps to relax a man
step outside its cold
snow on the ground cool brisk sound
the crunch beneath my boots as i bring in some more wood to keep your tuts
warm
i throw the logs on the fire the flame burst and sparks kick as i poke with a steel
stick
turn to the right to light the candle wick
so comfortable now but grab a towel and lets soak for an hour
the bubbles the rose peddles

the wine the bread the cheese the chocolate the fruit its all just another day with
love tucked in the boot carrying it where ever we go
its winter its cold so lets catch a plane and fly out of this rain
hit the beach the hot sand the cool breeze the sound of the waves and birds is
natures best ease
i wish every moment like these would just freeze
take a step back just stair breath in the air
walk around to catch the moments
now jump forward and keep it all in motion
i wish this was every day some sort of love potion
love is forever love is rare
love is true and it happened with you
i feel it now i felt it then
i want you here when i say when
youre away i pretend to be okay
i just wish tomorrow and everyday could fade a different way
not this way so i pray and i say that everything will be okay
we keep ourselves busy we travel we dance
we talk in a stylish stance but deep down we seek love and romance
when we have it its blind its just the wrong thoughts in ones own mind
but we do know that in our hearts and in our mind there is always space to allow
for time
time to heal time to feel
and time to kneel just to make it all feel real
i spend some lonely nights in the dark
closing my eyes open them but no surprise
so close my eyes through the ceiling and into the night starry skies
to see the north star and imagine the pictures in my eyes
i fall asleep to my own heart beat
wake up and look at my feet
turn up the music to start to a nice beat
open the fridge and pull out some breakfast meat
slice some fruit squeeze some juice
a shot of whisky now im feeling loose
a steamy shower for a half hour
look in the mirror and see the reflection of my dear
over my shoulder or before my face
i turn my back and enter the race
when does it end when does it begin
i dont know where im headed or when its time to win
but i do know its happening im going against the wind
my face forward and my hair flying back
everyone against me but no turning back
im confident im comfortable but its all soo unpredictable
so i run and run and jump into the pool
sink to the bottom like a heavy silver spoon

my clothes soaked heavy as stone
i float my self to the top so im sitting at the throne
a girl beside laying warm on a stone
i hear a moan she says where have you been
ive been waiting at home no where have you been
i was lost beneath the wind
she says the sun is shinning and the weather is warm
she touches my shoulder grabs my hand
 tells me to try and understand
for me you have to be that man
water turns dry to sand
its all too easy to understand
like gods own plan
no worries no fights no questions new advice
but between you and i its always been nice
like a soft sweet warm cinnamon spice
thats you thats us so lets stop all the fuss and know whats touched us

"Essence of Time"

time is precious at times im restless
many days and nights have touched us
what words to write what words to say
i dont wanna begin to push you away
only hope you come back each day
knowing it'll be okay
so i wait so i pray
it helps burry the pain away
my head up your head down
my face forward your back around
no sound a glance at your face side shown a frown
maybe i make you feel down maybe not let me turn you around
a smile a mile pumping my heart like a blood filled nile
is this love being preserved or just a crooked arrow that hit with a curve
a million reasons to stay a few you feel right away
though u decide to refuse it each n every day
leaving me the most to say but hearing it all will just push you away
all i ever wanted was our first day and love to stay
now i fall back and hit the floor because you walked out and hit me with the door
i thought i was a man that you adore
but only now my heart feels poor
as you are my lady that made me
made me grow to become a man
learn to change for a better man

trust me babe i truly do understand
dont turn it off like one button on a fan
or crunch it up like an old soda can
i could never do it that way
i wouldnt be that man
but only that man that you understand
the one you need because for you as a woman it is being me as man
and to know and feel i wish you could see and understand
but your back turned your head down
im not close enough now to turn you around
a smile or is it a frown
its a thought that leaves me down
with no sound the door is open your space is here
so dont pretend to disappear
i only wish you were near right up to my ear
lean in and tell me something i need to hear
baby please dont have fear you can run and have fun but in the end wheres your
number 1
for me its you and i dont need a clue
because ive always been stuck on you like glue
but me i must now be number 2
i ll wait for a few but dont think for a second i dont love you
but now i do need a clue and im getting nothing good from you
but for you good is all i can offer you
because you aint number 2 and i aint had a few
its only ever been you just
said the wrong things that pushed you away
when all i really wanted was love and our first day
but now your too far and i dont know what to say
nothing at all will that make it okay
i dont know but something tells me to do this every day
because you give it your all and if they walk away
theres nothing left to say but if its true it wont continue this heart broken way

"Flower"

a seed drops from a flower
hits the ground beneath the shower
shower of rain circulating around onto grain
a seed lay feeling no pain
no stain having no name
just knowing one day it will grow to fame
fame in a photo under ones nose
but for now it only grows
puddles aside the grass blows
bringing fresh hair up your nose

take a step you wont regret
your foot slips beneath your hips
you start to glide hit the ground and open your eyes
rain drops slow it down it's the most precious sound
each drop will hit the ground
pop plop stand up don't lay like a mop
hold your head high and brush your self off
keep up your walk and hear the dogs bark
as neighbors talk so near now your heart beats in your ear
up the step knock on the door let me in its starting to poor
we kiss we stand we hold each others hand
turn up the music of our favorite band
is it jazz classic salsa or something softa
all i know is we are here n i gotcha
its only the best feeling
so lets head to the kitchen and start peeling
dinners ready we sit we laugh we joke and blow out the candle leave before the smoke
head to the door open it up
no more rain just fresh air
a cool misty breeze lets go for a walk
the sun comes out one last time as it sits above the mountains behind
setting soon its now past nine
in our shadows it all looks perfect
no stains
no names
no pain
just two flowers growing from the rain
the sun is shinning so back to the fields of gold wheat and grain
that day i fell and felt no pain
something has grown there so lets give it a name
hold it under our nose whats your favorite name
because a baby is only the beginning and run of our family and name

DONT

Don't tell me if I'm dying I'd rather fall while I'm flying
Don't tell me what it says Id rather never know
Don't tell me how much time I never even knew
Don't wake me because I'm dreaming I'd rather live this way
Don't push me because I'm pulling I'd rather not fall over
Don't block the sun and shade me I need to feel alive
Don't close the window now I need to hear the rain
Don't turn the music down I want to feel the beat
Don't tell me because it hurts I've done all this before
Don't ask than interrupt I'd rather never say
Don't promise than give away I'd rather you just lie
Don't smile when it hurts I'd rather feel the pain
Don't turn your back on me ever my life is not a game
Don't pretend to understand and go behind my back
Don't be around me in this way, not even one more day
Don't try and help me ever if a favor will fall hard
Don't give me anything ever if it's just too damn hard
Don't try and be around me than push me up against the wall
Don't act like this is true and real let your self be free
Don't hide what really happened I'd rather know the truth
Don't hide the reasons ever I'd rather understand
Don't be who I want you to I love you for who you are
Don't lie it only upsets me lets not break our trust
Don't sit alone at night I'd rather comfort you
Don't be scared I won't be mad I will never reject or criticize you
Don't turn your back or run away I really do love you
Don't shake and shiver ever I coming to give you a hug
Don't give up when I'm angry or my mistake towards you
Don't forget my intention I'm only looking after you
Don't come and than go I'm losing all my hope
Don't tell me that you love me than do things to confuse me
Don't show me you don't love me than go to stand by my side
Don't give up or close your eyes my eyes are just for you
Don't give up and look elsewhere I'm everything you need
Don't fall down than run away I'm here to lift you up
Don't shed a tear with out me here I want to be that man
I will always stand up tall never shall I collapse nor never shall I fall
Sometimes goodbye is the only way but we're still alive
Sometimes hello is just so simple but we're way passed that
Don't ever fall and crawl never shall you collapse nor never shall you fall
I do all this to remember don't push our life away
If you don't love me now please just go away
You're in my heart forever but to you I'll fade away

Hope

I hope one day as I pray that love and trust will come my way
I hope at night what can't be seen is never ugly and never mean
I hope my friends and family close are true with love never hidden like a ghost
I hope my faith and trust in you is something important and valued by you
I hope my words and actions beat only to better each day we meet
I hope this life that leads my day gets better with age with out fading away
I hope everyday what I put out it easily taken in with out a shout
I hope one day as I pray strength continues to come my way
I hope with faith that love and trust fills my life and spreads like rust
I hope my faith and trust in you is in return coming from you
I hope like ivy all above spreads growing like flowers gliding like sleds

"WRECKLESS"

Wreckless endless forgiveness
trust this love this live this
breath this is us
this is love love is blind
don't leave it behind
open your eyes memorize
all surprise all nervous and butterflies
first kiss the look in our eyes
laying in bed fantasize
kids marriage worries aside
friends family live to lead our lives
a step ahead we are out of bed
gonna do it together smooth as a sled
wrong thoughts in the head
now only right words to be said
push it away under the bed
let seep beneath the dead
because its all been bled
maybe one day a lady to be wed
but first lets get past this stupid dread
its obvious who we are its obvious what we have
no more of this mess
no more complications
enough said no more stress
no more fuss
no more negative to ever touch us
angels over us god watching us
family and friends circle us
hand in hand together looking after us
together each other we take care of us
all of this all of us
you and I no reason to fuss
love is wreck less endless finds forgiveness
trust this love is faithful
love is truthful
space and time to find this and lies to complicate this
holidays near years passing by
life's to live alone we shall cry
but only if we continue to deny
marriage for kids marriage for wrong reasons
don't let love slip away fighting what's true making another lie now I begin to die
inside outside I cry doesn't make sense so stop the deny end the cry
hold each other for a moment and let the space pass by

together now knowing mistakes are to learn
change is for the better understanding respecting caring
listening teaching speaking giving writing expressing
holding touching loving is from one to another with love forever
we can dance we can laugh we can romance and travel in a prance
memorizing and holding each moment and each special glance
lets live life as our first dance it is the best feeling to have love and romance
this is life this is love this is us so lets circle the globe
around and around until we fall back in bed
a special place and time to where be wed
than laying in bed knowing family ahead
dreamy eyes of kids in bed
dancing around early mornings late nights
forgive and forget all the stupid fights
just dance just prance live our life's with each others love and romance.

AWAY

You shine like a sun over a garden
You rise like a flower in the soil
You fall gently down to the wind
I want to find you and hold you forever
I am here crawling on my knees
You are there hidden between the trees
You rise like a swan at dawn
You glide like a kite into the night
You shine like a moon over water
I want to pull you so to shine upon me forever
I am a shooting star falling on your lap
You are the pillow with me while I nap
You rise like a wave in the ocean
You fall gently down to the sea
You are the prettiest thing ever, I guess this is meant to be
I am here calling you down
You are the jet speeding faster than sound
You are away never to touch ground
You are like a bird the beautiful early morning sound
I wish to leave my window open
For everything I see and hear is the only way to which allows me to be near

"SUSU"

Suraya Aburaneh a lady not given away
with family she shall stay
arrest in bed she shall lay
one with class will always pray
nothing bad only good to say
fear no fear she is here
leaning close soft and near
sneaking up upon your ear
whispering words only good to hear
making you smile into the mirror
taking away all doubt and fear
pushing far what you don't want here
refreshing beauty is all too clear
only shows a joyous tear
a beauty stands inner to out
living life to what its all about
tall she stands no need to shout
success ahead no need to pout
focused on the perfect route
painting of you above the mount
soo many no need to count
what was in is now out
because susu said and that's all that counts
she is right you are wrong
so turn up her favorite song
hop aboard business in hong kong
real estate or dinner date
fashion show or out you go
sky diving hi fiving
living this life so reviving
breathing in what she breaths out
nothing skipt nothing left out
hit the water a yacht to the islands
publicist oh boy you wish
just going for a tropical dish
than back home im never alone
maybe not lets head to rome
my legs are crossed my clothes well worn
because I appreciate the day I was born
never torn never morn
making it through each day and storm
only to see the sunrises and suprises
looking forward to what arrises
my name is susu for those who knew for those who don't watch out I coming to surpass you

"LIGHT GIVES LIFE"

A match stick glides a rough strip
a train squeals at late night
chopped wood in a brick built hole
a wax candle sitting still
electricity is out a new bulb into the socket
a walking man with his lantern
the sun arises beyond the mountains
the lights appear beyond the trees
the star shoots in the night skies
the moon appears as the sun dies
a baby cries a mom opens her eyes
a bond fire in the country side
nature and manmade
reaction to action
controlling what we can
smells and memories come to mind
as light appears things come alive.

SHINNING DOWN

I know you're shinning down on me from heaven
I feel the warmth upon my back
I feel the strength you give me every day
With tears of depression I push my hopes away
I know you're here taking away all fear
In a dream I see your presence near
It is you that whispers softly, wind upon my ear
I know you try and tell me, everything will be okay
But day to day has hit me, I want to fade away
I know you're free living on
But with much pain I hate you gone
Everyday I miss you, for on one day I shall embrace you
For now you're shinning upon my face
A smile and tear, a winning race
With time and age I'm closer
Grey and frail I do grow older
For your tender heart I'm after
I know my heart and soul is yours
When heavens angels descend, please open up the doors

"SOMEONE EVERYONE STOP AND THINK"

Breath in breath out
stop and think what life is about
stand still be still
roll your head back what do you feel
close your eyes grab your thighs
what was lost realize
memorize let go
open your eyes
dark night starry skies
what lives always dies
ladies guys white lies
no surprise recognize
don't despise what you know
don't let go who you are
what you have today tomorrow have
no sorrow accept protect
recollect and collect
today now this minute you live.

"AFTER"

Heaven or hell
open your eyes to see the face of god
dust to wind our bodies become unknown
faces names like shadows into the night
only next day to move forward to a new light
than again into the night
alive than dead
do we become road kill
kicked to the side lights out a black out
a grain of sand on the beach
another star a million more to reach
into the dirt covering this earth
one hundred virgins what ever we want
billions of people walking above below or around this earth
present omnipresent always felt
always known dreams and reality
seeing thinking hearing and whispering
praying believing what is said
what we want what we know
sinking below
staying here drifting off a soul
an angel a guardian a person a horse
another organism a seed into dirt
a flower held against a shirt
a wave in the ocean a tree over one
a dial on a clock reflecting from the sun
can we love again can we live again for how long
with known faces or unknown
is it all new as nervous as the first day
or something warm and comfortable
like an ordinary day
this is the journey we live and risk we take
no answers only belief
left in a mysterious way
in control with confidence
or scared and worried what comes next
no fear its all clear
the same way we came here
we begin to open our eyes
begin to realize
we find a way a reason to stay
a way to live and the next shall begin the same
always comfortable with out fear adapting to what comes near.

"SLIDING ON THE WORLD"

I'm sliding on the world in a silk suit
my tie a tornado over my shoulder
my body turns twisting pulling fast and sudden
my butt aches my stomach in my throat
I can't breath I can't see
no sound no ones around
my laces untie my shirt buttons pop
my zipper breaks and my pants are up my crouch
my eyes big my mouth opened wide
I can't see so I close my eyes
I can't hear so I scream
I can't breath I pass out
awake in a tree a million feet tall
trying to climb down trying to fall
but it only grows tall
I am dreaming in a dream I climb to the top
than look down and see snow caps below
boots on my feet a cool brisk
I begin to slide slow to fast
down the hill over a frozen lake
under a polar bear into a tunnel
sitting on the tracks to which only a train travels
I hear the sound I see the lights
I feel the vibration jump to my feet
and hit the wall my body flat
my head to the side my cheecks feeling the pressure that brings my heart out of my chest
I grab the last poll bursting I go
grasping with all I have I swing behind with one hand and my finger tips
over a bridge I let go flying but under control
I soar low to high into the sky
looking down a snowy village the sun sets
the stars are out through the windows I see the candle light and fire bright
left to right feeling alive over the ocean my reflection big
I am a giant I am a beast
stepping my foot earth quakes ground brakes
volcanoes burst just another day sliding on the world

"THE ATHLETE BREATHES THE ATHLETE LIVES"

Every morning till dawn you're on the field
the grass is wet the air is damp
the sun is rising the weather cool
your muscles aching and body light
the smell of leather fresh cut grass
morning air hose water
BO and cotton all fill the air
setting off your senses memories and ambitions
tired but alert exhausted but in need
every day you are here
putting your all into every stretch
every sprint every step
and every breath
your heart pumps your skin sweats
every inch you fight and die
for every second you thrive and live for
every day carrying over the one before
you pace yourself and push yourself
leaving everything on the field
every day practice or game this is what you live for
this is what you're here for
the love the passion the rush the glory
the chills the cries the screams and chants
the team the coach the captain the stadium
the lights the whistles adrenaline pumping
blood rushing the faces the eyes the bodies the competition
this is why you're here it will never leave it will never go
you will live this and never let go
the butterflies the exhaustion triumph and battlefield
you will teach this and let everyone know
an athlete is in you so let it flow
let it show let it go
this is life this is you
so live now for the moment
leaving everything on the field
giving every day your all
win or lose you are victorious
you are an athlete you are letting all within come out
no holding back no mistakes
give it your all every day
looking back you are going to wish you did
do it now!

When We Are Together
When you close your eyes to go to sleep
When you shut off sound to hear my heart beat
When you lean in close to keep warm
When I feel your soft skin gently against mine
When I touch your face against my cheek
When I glide my hands through your hair
When I hold your hips and touch your thighs
When I kiss your lips to open your eyes
When you turn pulling my arm
When you shuffle back into mine
When you moan a sound of comfort and need
When you grab me pulling me close
When face to face we fill the space
When so close nothing between us
When body to body wrapped together
When we sleep we are together
When can we find more time to be together

September 11th The Day You Left
I long to see you everyday
Circled by you in every way
Though I am alone at night
I am circled by the sea of night

I wish to see your eyes again
Hoping this is all pretend
A dream is when my wish comes true
Dreaming seeing I'm holding you

Longing for this day
A sea of night a ray of light
An empty meadow cold September night
Upon your stone I shall lay

A single tear I shall pray
My head is bowed the flowers drop
A candle flickers the light is out
I stand to rise upon my feet
Walking away I close the gate

Walking away looking back
Wishing God would bring you back
Crying screaming shivering shaking
On the 11th this day you were taken

Stricken

You are stricken by words of anger
You are stricken by a hand of fear
You are grabbed tight than pulled near
You are crying shocked and full of fear
You don't know what to do you don't know what to say
Something happened to bring this day
Right or wrong immoral or a sin
Excuses and reasons shouting on and on
Some understand it's something that happens
Parents to children
Children to friends
Wife to husband
Husband to wife
Coach to player
Teacher to student
Player to teammate
We learn and forgive
Mistakes and regrets
True love and friendship always
My finger to your lips
Please do not say a word I know our mistakes
This is now so don't look back
Stricken by this day forever
That day I can't take back
This stricken day scared my heart forever
This day has changed us both forever
Time and space changing us forever
I wish this stricken day understood
I wish this stricken day accepted
I wish this stricken day forgiven
I wish this stricken day to better us both
I wish this stricken day would pass unnoticed
Both of us are stricken now surviving this we shall
Time and space will do this my love I hope you want the same
Like puppies we loved like animals we fought
Our love is priceless and can not be bought
Trust has come trust has gone
A bridge was built and walked upon
With love and trust we kicked the dust
We built a bridge so beautiful
We built our bridge together so strong resembling our lives together living on

What value does our bridge have
Never shall our bridge break
I shall always value thou
I wait the day to travel again
Hand in hand crossing our bridge
Hand in hand our back to the wind
Stars and sun upon our face
Refreshing waves upon our feet
Living our life together with love and trust so true
Memories moments passing by is only good with you
I hope to see the day again the day we first met
I hope to hold you when you want I wish you never went
I hope today like everyday we embrace each other strong
Living together knowing right from wrong

"LIVE NO MATTER WHAT"

I can't see today
I can't see tomorrow
but I will live today and I will live tomorrow
even if its going wrong you're running through my mind
you're running through my heart no matter what you say
no matter what you do I won't fall apart
I can't see today I cant see tomorrow
but I will live today and I will live tomorrow
you're catching my fall you're catching my breath
I'm still not breathing but walking with nothing left
I don't see you now I don't see you ever
but I will still love and live this life forever
I can't see today I can't see tomorrow
but I will live today and I will for ever live tomorrow
with or with out you my heart is beside you
nothing in life will ever deny you
my love is life and it will revive you
be who you are and it won't ever hide you.

"JUST GO"

Where did you go
why did you go
when and how where did it all go
why did you let go
I'm standing naked alone in the snow
like cupid an arrow in need of a bow
a kayak an ore in need to row
feel the ocean beneath me flow
my mind aside beside letting go
pulling pushing the tide shall know
questions answers yes or no
who shall know which way to go
only you answers you won't let go
leaving you alone no one to know
on top a rail set sail I go.

"THE POET"

Written to perfection these words to expression
every letter quick written
each word heart stricken
pushing to the right these words I type
pencil in hand gripped by a man
read by all I collapse and fall
arise with thoughts that set me back in my stall
a dungeon a place writing evening to dawn
soar alone like calices on palm
tough without nerves thoughts stand tall
running out of paper writing on a wall
feeling to short lean down I shall crawl
writing on floor than onto the door
filling up space a frown upon my face
on to a latter the chandeliers shatter
making room to enjoy my hand written platter
no light I write with eyes closed tight
no reading no speaking
just writing to enlighten the dungeon I shall brighten dusk to dawn I begin to yawn.

"TOUCH"

You touched my face so beautiful
you called my name so softly
you held me close so tightly
we burned with desire so warm
our hearts lit like fire so known
commitment untorn so worn
moments shared so adorn
making love our lives so reborn
you laying in bed my love so morn
you left me now my heart so torn

"ELEPHANT"

An elephant in a jungle covered in mud
a bed of water an eye so big and tusk so strong legs so long
a tail a swift left to right
a walk so seldom felt into the night
a smile so big looking so bright
only to stomp when entering a fight
only to run when ridden by a gun
villagers arms open together they run chasing an elephant is custom town fun
a pop a flop a bullet shall drop
an elephant has begun a journey covered in mud
a bed of water an eye so red
it lay and bled what can be done what can be said
this is a life chosen to be led one more elephant left to lay dead.

"WAR GOES ON FREEDOM LIVES ON"

War and peace at home and in the streets
we shout we fight they surrender into the night
1 pilot 1000 lay dead
1 gun 1000 lay dead
1 bomb 1000 lay dead
1 life 1000 lessons to be said
nothing heard they fight ahead
some come home others starve unfed
skinny to bone 1000 lay dead
songs of freedom moments unread
bullets passing as there guns are blasting like fire flies into the night the sky
soo bright hitting windows with might
kids adults scream in fright
parents families dream and pray its alright
only to see and hear all through out the day and night
reasons excuses with meaning they fight
some understand and feel it's alright
some protest blaming pointing in anger they yell and fight
no matter what is done it's all a balance of something not right
but sitting here with out fear being able to write
in all ways we do our best to make it through this fight
to live another day and dream another night
hoping to find peace and end war would be right.

"COFFEE SHOP DAY DREAMING"

Coffee shops music and road blocks
homeless and flip flops
copper tins pennies in dens
office pants old leaking pens
pigeons chickens and old mother hens
family love and social friends
cats and dogs scratching at our shins
ones own mind blowing up the winds
shattering glass motels and holiday inns
failing to lose one only wins
hanging up first place ribbons with gold rusted pins
smoking and sucking down bottles and gins
church confessions life and sins
tacos and chips in old tortilla bins
fish and sharks make soups with fins
lights are bright knob dims
left to right they look like twins
heat fire blazing in metal kin's
singing and ranting one pretends
ocean seas and beach winds
sand towers beneath the boardwalk
splinters and pork shops
beach fries vinegar and salty eyes
crunchy sandwiches and watery eyes
sunburned skin and lotion downed thighs
bright blue skies
night sticks purple kicks
fire flies
top down one only drives
running to the beach jumps and dives
hot to cold dry to wet
sharks dolphins fear and no fear
shallow to deep I awake from my sleep.

RELAX

My back arest my feet swollen
My legs sore my eyes closed
My head back my hands behind
Alone I sit in silence in dark
The window open the screen shut
The cool breeze and cricket sounds
The moonlight and starry skies
The dark woods and grassy fields
No more aching no more pain
I sit relaxed at peace at ease
I enjoy nature while the world sleeps

OLD MAN

Skin like leather tough from the weather
Hair thin with a familiar scent
Wrinkles with age like a tree and its rings
Feeling shorter feeling frail
Not much color turning pale
Friends and family not around
Feeling young looking old
Inside a boy outside a man
With time came age wisdom in hand
A shot of scotch a cigar and chair
Sitting rocking a fire a glare
A creaking of wood as old as I
Do you know me look into my eye
Can you hear me listen to my voice
Can you feel me read what I write
Imagine being young and one day being old
How slow how fast time can go
How good how bad will it flow
How long how short only god will know
Today tomorrow Im letting go
An old man dies a baby cries
One life ends a new begins

BY AUTUMN DAY BY AUTUMN NIGHT

By autumn day by autumn night I sit with eyes closed so tight
The sun is shinning oh so bright my curtains mustn't be closed right
The heat upon my face sets in my pale skin now red again
By autumn day by autumn night I sit alone in dark in fright
The room is empty cold and bare as night sets in I sit and stare
My curtains closed but bright in light because the moon sits upright
The light of day and light of night keeps me under a spot light
Beams of light from day to night shinning oh so damn bright
I sit and stare naked and bare this fight from light mustn't be right
By autumn day by autumn night the colorful leaves uplifting and bright
By autumn day by autumn night shadows and colors from day to night
By autumn day by autumn night I sit outside with out a fight
By autumn day by autumn night I realize the beauty in light
By autumn day by autumn night family and friends a circle so tight
Night to day I am happy to stay leaves shall fall as I grow tall

THE LAST HELLO GOODBYE

We met one day and stayed all night
A soft hello a kiss goodnight
One night rolls over one day arises
Hearing your voice my heart realizes
Letters and gifts best surprises
To stay all day and stay all night
Feelings you bring words so right
One day one night never shall fight
From night to day we shall lay
Sunday church we shall pray
Side by side we shall stay
Knowing one day far away
A last hello a last goodbye
In a dream beyond the gates
Another day another night
Together in hand because we wed

PIRATES ABROAD

We see the sun has gone to sleep knowing now the moon shall creep
A pack of sheep together they sleep the wolves are on the prowl
Sounds of man now arrest nature shall come alive
The pine trees tall but black and white sitting beneath the light

The moon is round with a face so bright a smile over our night
A man asleep an open eye a pillow full of weapons
One foot in the other out sleeping he only pretends
Nestled in the hills far out now getting ready to head out

A trade he enters for what is right most don't understand
He can sit and fight day and night or act an average man
No matter what is said or done he continues with his plan
Crossing lines below above fast and slow he moves

Mixing in and disappearing like a wind upon our face
This man a smuggler with in a pirate an underworld in need
Supplying what is in demand only good deals in deed
Taking risk with out fear each days a moment so unclear

No thoughts or worries ever a pistol beneath my rear
If I wasn't good at this I wouldn't be standing hear
Today has past set sail at last for a new day is near
Respect and honor always, family shall come first

Never shall one be harmed, always reacting unarmed
In self defense I shall commence only to escape
A smugglers life a chosen life never shall we weep

Passing By

Life is a beautiful death a succession of battles fought to a death
Poetry in motion is images drawn out words beautifully spoken
A poet's pen dipped in ink expressed on carvings from a tree
Brass beds with cold sheets flickering candle light

A flask a glass a shot of scotch a poor boys hat only Irish knit
Smoking pipes tobacco leaves ash and raspy voices
Spectacles blackened by the flame a shadowed painting
Wine splattered into glasses broken bottles spilled paint

The horses racing a gentleman speaking a lady passes by
Lipstick on a napkin telling white lies only innocence of a lie
Children below the knee, in mother's hand they stand
Lining fields of gold a dusty dirty road

Cotton grows linen spreads a clothing line hangs low
A colorful butterfly opens its wings wind and seas a soft breeze
Hay in the back of a pick up truck rusty and loud it moves
Beauty Greed filth and need tempt and test desires in deed

Wealth at hand rich and poor a penny lays on heads
A silver dollar in the air flipping spinning it lands
Echoing in the open ceilings, silver to marble, a smack
Throwing marbles shooting dice gathering jacks

Paper money paper planes cardboard games
An old man sits a young boy stands eating chocolate with dirty hands
Tears in an old mans eyes a smiling sunrise
A young boy with Irish eyes chocolate hits the floor

An old man with missing teeth bends to pick it up
Gathering jacks chocolate bars and everything at his feet
An old man taking all he can his life has passed him by
Passing by day and night living life nothing right

Today you saw a man whom yesterday a boy
An ugly birth a beautiful death Life's a broken toy
Force a smile chuckle a laugh living this life to find the joy
Once alive now arrest you are no longer the boy

A broken toy an innocent lie a succession of battles is life passing by
An ugly birth a beautiful death a ship wreck or set to sea
Live this life as you are free taking honey from the hive stinging just to stay a live
Like a turtle on its back suffering from no control

Unanswered questions curiosity and doubt kills your soul
Trust the life you live or lead the life you trust filling an empty bowl
Putting dust behind you clearing what's in front of you continuing as you go
This is just a simple life passing as you go

"Poetry & expression written to make a change"

"A view into our world"

"Our children are our future"

"Written expression is poetry in motion achieved without rules, limitations or editing"

"Love is life-Give it trust-What we make of it is meant to be-We all have choices-Put yourself where you see yourself-How you live is up to you-Stop and think-Now decide"

"Refreshing Freedom"

$1 *for every book sold will be donated to* war torn *countries*

Written & Original by; **Geoffrey S Hyde**

www.ingramcontent.com/pod-product-compliance
Lightning Source LLC
Chambersburg PA
CBHW060058050426
42448CB00011B/2523